QUIET
NOISE
Poems, Affirmations
& Intimate
Thoughts
Paul Haynes
as Dhoruba
Kali

INTRODUCTION

"Noise is noise, at any decibel. Whether soft, loud, or even inaudible… it's all the same. Vocalize with a purpose."

Katina Davis-McCoy

For most of my life, I have been labeled "the Quiet One." Whether it was at home, school, church, or work – anywhere! Not only is my voice soft and low, but my demeanor and personality have always maintained a composed, humbled, or reposed state. Yet, I slowly came to the realization (as have all my blood brothers) that when we talk, people listen. I mean really listen! Not only do they listen, but they feel an overwhelming comfortability in sharing their life stories and situations with us. It was the very same way with our father, Rev. John Haynes, Jr.

Understand that this is no small matter; when you are imparted with the wisdom and supernatural ability to be an empath, that load becomes heavy at times. HOWEVER!!! The rewards of seeing and knowing that you have spiritually, physically, emotionally, and mentally helped someone else are immeasurable. Even in being nicknamed (and fully embracing) a "quiet storm;" and at times hard to hear, I have learned that I still have something to say! Whether vocally or in scribe, my thoughts and words, guided by a Supreme and Infinite Intelligence, are meant not only to be heard, but felt. Even in the hush of twilight and the whisper of dawn, within the gentle cadence of life's unspoken emotions, lies a world of quiet storms and noise.

This collection of poetry invites you to embark on a journey through the landscapes of the heart and soul, where emotions surge like hidden tempests beneath tranquil surfaces. Each verse is a raindrop, a lightning flash, an ode to the intricate symphony of human experience. As you turn these pages, may you find solace amid life's tumult, and may you discover the beauty that emerges when moments of introspection collide with the passions that reside within. Like a storm that sweeps away the debris, these poems delve deep, seeking to cleanse and renew, to inspire and uplift. They are a testament to the resilience of the human spirit, reminding us that even in the quietest storms, there is strength, growth, and the promise of brighter skies beyond.

With these words, this book is meant to inspire and give insight; as well as ignite passions and life purpose. To get you in the mood for whatever your emotional occurrence is at any given time; to become mindful and present in whatever noise reverberates within your Youniverse. Inspiration and motivation are my light... and positivity is my oil. I pray this book entertains you, but more importantly, that it helps and builds you, meeting you at your desired level of artistic satisfaction.

DEDICATIONS

This book is dedicated to all my ancestors who have transitioned from this life…

To my father, thank you for all your teachings and wisdom and helping to form my foundation in this world. For being an example! A father figure to so many and enlarging our "family." You are forever missed and loved.

To my grandparents, aunts, and uncles whom I never got the chance to meet (John Haynes, Sr., Ethel Haynes, Robert Davis, Mary "Patsy" Haynes Drake, Marvin Davis and Robert Davis, Jr.); and to those who helped to raise me (Charlie "Pop" Barnett, Odell Barnett, Beulah Marie Davis, Joseph Guy Davis, Aileen Haynes Jacobs, Marion Haynes, Claxton Johnson, Sr., Ricky V. Haynes, beloved cousin Ethel Mae Haynes Wilson); more recently, my dear sister (now soul sister), Katina Davis-McCoy and my dear sweet cousin, Anita Johnson– I carry your torch and baton through this life marathon.

Wherever you are, may our Creator and your spirits continue to guide and mold me into greatness.

THANK YOU

A very special thank you to my mother, Phyllis Haynes, for all her Love, and never-ending support. For her part in my foundation formation, and transcending her gentle, loving, and kind spirit into me so that I could truly have a balanced internal ecosystem. I love you more than anyone and anything in this world!

To my wife, Danielle, thank you for your unconditional Love, understanding, and support. Despite my shortcomings, and sometimes, short sightedness, your unwavering dedication to us and helping to build and secure our future is a jewel I will always treasure! I love you!

To all my family – We're definitely EVERYWHERE and extraordinaire! Thank you all for who you are and the impact you have made in/on my life. To my sisters and brothers, "Strong Seven," we were molded in explicit Greatness! Let's do our part to ensure it was not in vain! Jo'sef, thank you for the book title. Katina, thank you for the opening quote that I borrowed and was inspired by.

Mrs. Shirley George, Mrs. Barbara Valery, Amanda Eaddy McKeithan, and Mrs. Wanda Williams – thank you for believing in me since day one; and the constant push and motivation to get published. True examples of strong, melanated, female educators and necessary women in our culture.

To Mrs. Rosa Edwards and Mrs. Zella Barnett – the melanated educators who taught and groomed me to be proud of my heritage, constantly reminding me that I AM SOMEBODY; and two of the first to see the leader in me. To those teachers and counselors who stood with them, ensuring a bright future for young boys and girls of color – Mrs. Sarah Robinson, Mr. Tom Stahl, Mrs. Kay Doto, Mrs. Adelaide Picart, Mrs. Susan Anderson, Mrs. Beverly Anderson, Mr. Howard Langford, Mrs. Wanda Peterson, Ms. Tania Gibbs, Ms. Sandra Willie, and Ms. Carol Reisinger. Thank you all for adding to my foundation… and for all the Snickers bars and blow pops!

Mrs. Eileen Frey and Mrs. Deborah Erskine – thank you for sparking the creative writer in me in the 8th and 12th grade, respectively. You were significant forces in pushing me to expand my mind artistically.

Ms. Christine "The Queen" Washington and Kinloch "Ghetto Chronicles" – a very huge thank you to these two who mentored and took me under their wing when I started performing spoken word. I'm forever indebted to the Something to Say poetry group in Charleston, SC for allowing me to expand and express my voice and thoughts. Thank you to the Queen, whom I admire very dearly for her work ethic, her poetic prowess and strong civic duties; for always pushing and believing with positivity.

In humble gratuity, thank you to all whose path I have crossed, for whatever reason and season. For the lessons learned along the way, I am truly grateful!

TABLE OF CONTENTS

Sound Byte 2 – Amplitude

Sound Byte 3 – Crescendo/Climax

Sound Byte 4 - Transformation

Energy Affirmation

I affirm that I am receiving, allowing, and accepting all that I AM and all that I AM becoming!

I AM at peace with who I AM...

I AM harmonizing my masculine and feminine into wholeness, melded with vulnerability, and no longer see the need to conform to societal ideals that have no true resonance with my heart.

I allow cosmic wisdom to trickle down and seep into my spiritual self, gracing me with illumination...

I AM honing my intuition to allow me to find the right situations and relationships that harmonize well within me for the next stage of my growth, and that support me going forward to manifest my highest potential and well-being on all levels.

I AM in the Flow of All That Is...

I AM fluidity...

I HAVE a deep, symbiotic relationship between my soul and Source...

I attract the abundance that is needed to live a life of fulfillment!

I release my personal burdens and traumas and accept my innocence. I forgive myself (say 3x)

Sound Byte 1: Tranquility

Imperfect Masterpiece

You don't have to be perfect for me
Your perfect imperfections are good to see
Because they let me view your humanity
And gaze at God's creation of beauty

You don't have to be perfect me
Why? How much of an imbalance would
that be?
Why should I have to strive to catch up to
you?
Knowing I could never pay the price it's
due...
Fighting a false war we both know is a
loss in lieu

We fall, we rise, we fall again. Such is
life...
But knowing we're in this together
soothes most of the strife
If we were made to be perfect, God
wouldn't have made us from dirt
His best resources he chose to subvert;
Yet His most precious tool He did assert

You don't have to be perfect for me
You don't have to be for yourself, either
We are a progression of maturity
Constantly learning and building; being
each other's receiver

You were made from the most precious
Your faults being a byproduct
Of a work of art in progress -
magnificently breathless
...and that in itself, baby, is at least a
start towards perfection

Forgive Me: A Poem of Redemption

I'm sorry I've disappointed you time and time again
Hurting your feelings, when in my mind is where the hurt began
Where it stays and I try to bottle it up
Yet it seeps out, and oozes to your heart... damn, that's fucked up

I shudder n cringe at the look in your face
Knowing your happiness has been indirectly replaced
By confusion, doubt, and mortal pain
I just wanna bring your smile back again

What you said to me, hurt me to my heart
But what I did was sufficient reason to part
And you're the one person I'm really not trying to lose
Eventually getting to the point of exchanging "I do's"

I know I need work, know I need time
Please bear with me... don't leave me behind
Trust me to keep your heart in my possession,
Trust me to love you until the end of this life lesson

Beauty

Beauty...
The beauty I see is not measured by size
It can't be covered by makeup nor by copy can it be plagiarized
Confidence seeps thru your attitude, and radiance thru your smile
Your walk is with prowess and seduction, bringing elegance to your sense of style
Beauty...
One of a kind to me you are... a 1st place prize.
How I wish you could view the way I see you, through my eyes
Never are you thought to be honorable mention
But I always honorably mention you in conversation and compliment
As one of the Creator's greatest masterpieces that He personally sent
Endowed with graceful features of a Nubian Queen
Partaking in true humbleness that surpasses the serene
Your touch is the ebb n flow tide to my chiseled face
Your kisses are like rejuvenating waters when on my lips they're placed
Beauty...
Summing up the definition of that plain and simple word

You give life and bring action, transforming that adjective, to a verb
Flowing effervescently through all your crevices and curves,
You embody Beauty as if on a well prepared dish waiting to be served
Even more so, waiting to be heard
That melodious tune of the sweetest songbird
Beauty...Baby...SexyLove...Sweetness...

Shit! To me, they're all da same word

While You Sleep

I watch you while you sleep
In wonderment and amazement
That you are mine, and I am yours
Every breath you inhale I pray is deep
Showing your body's peaceful fulfillment
A tally of the day's work, catching up to work's score

I watch you while you sleep
Sometimes not touching you or making a peep
But snap shooting mental pics with my eyes
Zooming and focusing on God's gifted prize
Admiring His craftwork, appalled by His artistry
Crafting someone of poise, grace, and intellect... just for me
And she lays next to me every single night
Caramel complexioned skin; and four voluptuous mounds in sight

I watch you while you sleep
Sometimes fighting the fatigue that creeps
Ignoring the heavy eyes that seemingly seep
Watching over you as a guardian angel's duty

Realizing right next to me is a real-life
Sleeping Beauty

Every night, I fall asleep with the moon
and stars on my chest
Every morning the sun rises in my face...
morning glory at its best
As I kneel to smell your flower bed, roses n
lilies in blossom;
Your morning dew soaks my lips; and all
previous pains go numb
I lay in the shade of your bosom as you
caress my head
Your soft and gentle touch got me
thinking of going back to bed
But I choose to stay up and take in this
glorious view...
This lovely masterpiece of natural
beauty... that is you

GOALS

Never forget how beautiful you are
Never discount the goals set afar
Day by day, take your time to remind
Yourself that you're never ever on rewind.
But ever moving forward towards your much anticipated prize
That look of success you see in the mirror, looking back at you
with your own two eyes
With every step, your spirit will rise,
Chasing dreams, reaching for the skies.
Embrace the journey, both lows and highs,
For within your heart, the fire never dies.
In the tapestry of life, you'll leave your mark,
A testament to courage, even in the dark.
Each challenge faced, a chance to embark
On the path to greatness, where dreams embark.
So never forget how beautiful you are,
A radiant soul, a shining star.
With perseverance, you'll travel the distance
And reach the goals you've set, in due instance.

My Life

Neva thought you'd get fed up,
Neva thought you'd just get up
And leave without a word... in silence.
Leaving a dark void... grim n tense
I see I hurt you emotionally n mentally
Thru my silence and not saying I'm sorry
Forgive my inconsiderate lack of care,
For my ignorant ability to be aware
Of just how precious you are to me...
Like the last breath I breathe,
Or the last light of day I see
Or a drop of water in the middle of a dry desert sea...
You are my heart beat, my joy in pain
My comfort, my peace, my sensible sane
Treasuring you as the Queen by my side
My thoughts or concerns I no longer hide
No matter how big or small, no matter the ease or strife
I'll share it all with you, my right hand... because YOU ARE MY LIFE!

Faded Pictures

Thought we'd get to spend a lil bit of time together
Seeing we really don't get time nowadays
Times have really changed and it's crazy that
This wonderland wasn't just a fixated craze
We're so close yet there's a strange distance
How can we bridge that? How can we mend this?
All the answers... the key lies within your heart
It's up to you of whether you want a brand-new start
I've already began this race, yet it seems I began alone
Looks like a picture once made of flowers have now turned to stone
A cold piece of steel, an unforgiving sharp blade
Pierces my eyes like the sun with no clouds... no shade.

Simple Things

Sometimes the words never need to be said
And being in front doesn't always mean you're ahead
A simple hand hold sometimes speaks the loudest
It's in those moments where you make me proudest
Because that one small action overpowers any word,
It resounds more loudly in my heart, yet never heard
Just want you to know your smile and touch is all I need
To keep pushing for our love; a true love story indeed!

Charleston Battery

Strolling along the Battery viewing and
listening to the sounds of the ocean
Taking in the sights and sounds of that
true poetry in motion
Wrapped in tranquility, the waves got me
captured and cloaked in
Like a witch's spell, I'm entranced by a
meticulous sea salt potion
Winds carry these thoughts to and fro
Tossed thru the air with really nowhere to
go
Pondering on the pounding this water
makes on these rocks
Sounds the same as the feeling in my
heart, like a ship crashing at the docks
Time inevitably passing... tick... tock
Looking in the distance at the horizon, its
distance is appealing
More so than these close shores next to
me, proximity got me reeling
Needing to go as far out and as deep down
as some of these anchors... that abysmal
feeling
But I can't stay here in this type of state
Gotta regroup and refresh this mind before
it's too late
Let these impoverished negative thoughts
abate
Let this natural scene appease my senses
at a quickening rate

Remember When…

Remember when I first told you I loved you?
That feeling inside that struck a colorful hue?
A brightness, a refreshing statement that rang true?
Remember when I first rubbed the soles of your feet?
It was an outward expression that our soles (souls) were bound to meet…
Rubbing away the past heartache and sorrow
Giving soothing hope towards a brighter tomorrow
Or our first kiss? It was so much more than physical bliss
A fairy tale that seemed like a happily ever after that the author missed
Remember when we vowed Bonnie and Clyde?
A time where our hearts chose not to hide
The true love we found and never wanted to subside
The realness, the happiness, the peace in which we could confide
Remember when we lived free from the cares of the world?
Slowing down to our level of living; in the circle of "us" we'd curl

Remember when we used to talk until
black midnight turned to blue?
Such precious and timeless moments I
remember... just wondering... do you?

Time

What do you do with time?
Does it bask in actions of sublime?
Do you let it pass by with regret?
Or tend to let it be an old wound you forget?
Maybe you toss it back and forth in your mind
Wishing it would fast forward or rewind
Keeping tabs on it like a team's score...
Or treat it like a lotto ticket, wishing you had more
Maybe it's like a drawn-out game you play,
Or perhaps you treat it like death, and it just slips away.
Do you treat it as if it's on your side
Like Nationwide?
And hold on to it with an impeding pride
Let it roll back and forth like an ebbing tide...
Knowing it's one thing you can't get back
And most certainly a treasure we all lack
Is your time used for the NOW moment?
Or in dwelling in the past or future of oblivious torment?
Moving in seconds, minutes, hours, days...
Either with cleared vision, or blurred haze
Time is something we all need to get under control and lock

For whether it’s with lightning speed or
sluggish pace, it still moves
Tick .... Tock

Black Wombman

First of humanity, giving birth to nations
Made from particles of universal oblations
Dipped in melanin's power of ethereal sensations
Formed by the cusps of the Creator's adulations
You are the Queen of mankind, you came before time
And are the reason I profess this rhyme
I bow in your presence and worship the ground you walk
I praise you for your subtle intuition and the wisdom you talk
Because you bring intuition to balance the logic
A sixth sense naturally implanted to lodge this
Knowledge and wisdom into every seed planted
Birthing new Queens and Kings; the access to royalty already granted
Different shades of brown, such a colorful hue.
Entranced by the dark, light, red, caramel, and honey skinned tones of your voodoo.
Some say you're God incarnate, which may be sacrilegious;
That's only because you're the first of the human race... indigenous.

Your light impedes the darkness of this world
Bringing beauty and hope; at all obstacles you are hurled.
Yet, your delectable disposition is unmoved and unphased
Challenges are wrought, yet you're never dismayed
Strength exceeding the physical and mental maze
And you wonder why these eyes stare at you in an amazed gaze
Why these hands run up and down your body with praise
Or why these thoughts try to describe you with the perfect phrase
Blessed is the Queen whose skin is of the night
That melanated glory whose sacred treasure gives light;
Who strengthens a whole nation by bearing just one child, in plight
Into a world she knows he or she will forever fight!

Growing Up Early

The 90's...
Hip hop and R&B at its apex
When music, ink and I became
A regular ménage trois...
Quiet and reserved, always observing;
Listening to the grown folks
Outside was an oasis, a treasure
Loved playing with umpteen cousins
But took in nature's kodak moments
An old soul in a teen's pubescent shell
Eager to earn a living...
Damn, should've held off on that part
Signed my life away to Uncle Sam in the end
Teen life...

Nature's Sweet Tunes

As the shores and sunset strum their melodious melody,
My soul sways in the wind, toes sunk in sand – earthen and watery.
The crescendo of the waves, the whisper of the clouds
To my heart through my ears does this natural orchestra endow.
Steady my breathing, giving meditation;
Focus my sight, without any dilation
One chord striking after another... no hesitation.
Rhythmic sensations
I feel beyond free!
The culmination of the Creator's artistry!
Acoustic tapestry
My five senses in utter glee
As the shores and sunset strum their melodious melody.

Tomorrow - A Triolet

Tomorrow is always a positive thought
Never promised, but always looked
forward to

Always up in the air, it gets caught
Tomorrow is always a positive thought
Hopes, dreams, and optimism wrought
Promises of what to say and do

Tomorrow is always a positive thought
Never promised, but always looked
forward to

An Ode to Emily

I have awakened! Back to reality!
My soul has transcended back to originality!
But I'm still here, my children, my grands
In legacy, in laughter, in fresh and distant memory.
Don't cry, mourn, nor weep for me –
Instead, be joyful that I'm now pain free
No longer shackled inside this human body;
But emancipated into ancestral immortality!
A part of the fabric that knits earth to the heavenlies!
If you should reach out for me,
I'll be there in some form or entity.
Maybe a rainbow... or some sweet melody.
A gentle breeze... or a little brown Bunny;
Or maybe a butterfly, a sure sign of serenity.
However, or wherever, you'll know I've left
a piece of me with each of you... surely.
So do not cry, mourn, nor weep for me –
For I'm now that thread woven intricately into eternity.
I will forever be Emily!
Sending sweet kisses to all of my family!

With deepest Love, Affection, and Sympathies for my

First cousin, once removed: Emily Haynes Brown

Just Breathe

Breathe...
I've held my breath for so long, I almost forgot
Its simplicity and automatic response.
Trying to stop, steer, and hold in the pains;
Thinking if I could control the life reins,
Then I'd master the emotional stains.
Breathe...
Possible damage from lack of oxygen
Mental scars
Cerebral jail bars
Brain cell wars
Breathe...
I need that refreshing!
That problem solving addressing!
That CPR, back to life, back to reality pressing!
Breathe...
Resuscitation
Breathe...
Steady dilation
Breathe...
Lost hopes' annihilation
Breathe...
Life revitalization
It can all be put back together,
It can all be ok if I just find shelter;
It can all start over from just a small sign of life;

It can all begin again without the strife
I just need to... <inhale> <exhale>
BREATHE!!!

REFLECTIONS

I looked in the mirror and saw a reflection;
But that person was now foreign to me.
Funny thing is, my soul was not in
objection
Because it realized I was only looking at
what I used to see.

His eyes were merely dull embers,
Compared to my fiery ocular stare.
His lips remained sealed and locked out of
fear tremors;
Seemingly, an embarrassing site to bear.

I used to lay waste to THE truth
Because at the time it all seemed so
fictional.
But the truth only appeared to be uncouth
Due to tales passed down with strict
adherence to traditional.

My reflection was no longer mine...
It was that of a different space and time
When I had been selfishly unkind
To the Merkabah within and led my third
eye blind.

When my instincts and gut did not line up
with my actions...
Feeling like I had to please certain people
and factions

Long denying self-satisfaction
And lured by the many distorted distractions

The real me cried out from the time that had been wasted;
But my reflection reached out and shook its feeble finger, "No."
In the same instance I raised my fist and laced it
With unapologetic black power – adjusting my crown to go.

My reflection formulated a smile of contentment and pride;
I was able to push past the fears and pain it couldn't do!
Our joy we both could no longer hide...
And in my mind, we both screamed, "Thank YOU!"

The Garden Nani*

The art and love of reciprocity can be
found in gardening.
The gifting – the taking – the sowing –
the reaping...
An effervescent cycle of continuous love,
care, and bountiful mutual benefits.
For this, I am Nature's Nurturer.
And my garden extends beyond my four
walls...
Beyond my backyard sanctuary...
Beyond my physical embodiment.
Tilling the soil with my hands;
Tilling the child's mind with education
Absorbing the nutrients within while
simultaneously planting seeds.
Nature's Nurturer – giving back what was
given to me by the Creator
In hopes that in return, Nature will
become the Nurturer
Once the Nurturer becomes one again
with Nature.

*To my Aunt Marion – I love you, forever!

Recipe of Love (Ode to Phyllis Ann)

A dash of discipline mixed with copious
amounts of wisdom and understanding
Preparation of a broad dish compassion
that never seems to cease expanding
Seven cups of joyfulness blended with
seven pounds of grace
Is sure to glean a smile of gratitude from
anyone's face
When the universe chose to put this
woman in the mix
Intricately weaving together two of the
most vital characteristics
The blissful culmination of servanthood;
The epitome of global motherhood –
It formed an ever-abundant superpower of
unconditional LOVE!
Certainly a tough cookie to break; this
mold, only God knew what it was made of
From the time you have carried your own
children in the womb,
You became a crisis interventionist,
standing guard against any impending
doom
Perfectly balancing the ingredients of faith
and karma –
Today, we can stand here proudly and
shout, "That's OUR Momma!"
As we reflect and honor you today, and
attempt a moment in history to capture;

Know that your retirement is not the end, but in fact, the beginning of a new chapter.
Delved in adventure... laced with event horizons of life's fulfilling wonder!
So charge full speed ahead with a blaze of lightning and thunder!
You have given a lifetime of servitude, and it hasn't all been sweet;
But now, it's past time for you to be served – so we say to you – BON APPETIT!!

Flashback Friday

Wishing in time I could go back
To when people had soul, jack!
Not the rhythmic flow, style, and dance pack...
But before our minds were invaded with coke and crack

When raised fists and oratorical speech were our weapons...
Where Earth, Wind, and Fire album covers subliminally spoke to the heavens.
When we bled, sweated, and cried of Black pride!
And stood in the gap for our elderly and children... for each other, side by side.

Destinies were sought after; all had purpose
Knowledge being ravaged instead of deemed worthless
Damn I wish I could go back... back track and never lack
In fulfilling the ancestor's wishes...
And that's a cool fact, jack!

Tidal Waves

It's said this moon is a natural satellite;
So I project my thoughts and desires
toward the skies
In hopes that the universe will align with
my energy and light
Reciprocating and duplicating my soul ties
From one receiver to another, Eye see you,
and welcome your donation...
Your lunar vibration
And emotional escalation
Thru tidal intonations
My zodiac resonates with your alignment!
Shifting with purpose and intent
Move me, baby...

A Dream Deferred

Sidelined – I put it all on the side and tried to hide
Whether to proceed with this greatness, I couldn't decide
Because I chose to put your dreams first an at the forefront
What difference would it make, if we were on the same hunt?
On the prowl like Mufasa and Sarabi
Making both our dreams our everyday hobby
But just like Langston's, it dried up like a raisin in the sun
No longer was it fun
The excitement was way past done.
Until I realized our dreams were separate
Opposite ends of the spectrum
Where they both were neglected
Feelings got involved and dissected
And those dreams somehow got disconnected
But I'm moving forward
And steady going toward
My goals and visions of self-enrichment
Steady looking for the hidden hints
That's meant to steer me towards excellence
So, regardless of what you thought or heard,

My dream didn't really die; it just got deferred.

Forward (FourWord)

There's only one direction that's safe and
sure
Only one direction that's bound to be pure
All others are tainted with distraction and
lure
This sickness of side, half, and back
stepping has a simple cure.
If I take Depression Blvd, shit's bound to
be hard;
That way seems never ending... too damn
far
And I need to stay alert and on guard.
Anger Avenue is nothing new
But I'm seriously not feeling the U-
Turn, heading back to Misery Street
Rather hitchhike on my own two feet
Damned GPS – This version I'll have to
delete.
Directions, for some reason, are on repeat.

Gotta move FORWARD towards progress
And not second guess!
Alleviate the stress!
De-clutter the mess!
Organize and plan the success!
Put optimism to the full test! AMEN!
So it now becomes a testAMENt!
Not left, not right. Not even to higher
heights

Just FORWARD motion toward the bright lights
Keeping faith and hope well within my sights
And each step taken, my soul awakens
No time for braking... I said no time for breaking!
Yep! Both of these, I'm eternally forsaking
Blowing all negativity a goodbye kiss
Chanting my mantra in repetitive bliss –
I CAN DO THIS!
I CAN DO THIS!
I CAN DO THIS!

In the spirit of the Ongwehonweh (original people) and guided by the ancestral wisdom of the Aniyunwiya (real or principal people), let this affirmation serve as a beacon of strength, unity, and harmony for Indigenous, Autochthonous, Black people. Rooted in the principles of the Great Law of Peace, we affirm:

"We stand as stewards of the land and guardians of the water, embodying the resilience and courage of our ancestors. In our hearts flows the love for our communities, as vast and deep as the rivers that nourish the earth. With every breath, we speak our truths, resonating with the force of the winds that sweep across the mountains.

We embrace freedom, not just as the absence of chains, but as the presence of dignity, the right to live our lives according to the sacred customs passed down to us. In peace, we find our greatest strength, a serene force that binds us, allowing us to grow together, like the great forests that stand tall and unwavering.

Justice guides our steps, a light that illuminates our path, ensuring that we walk in balance with all creation. We honor the Great Law of Peace, the ultimate expression of harmony, respect, and equity. This law reminds us that true power lies not in dominion over others, but in the collective prosperity of all beings.

Today, we affirm our commitment to live by these principles, to uphold the legacy of those who came before us, and to forge a future where every voice is heard, every life is valued, and every action contributes to the healing of our world.

Let this affirmation be a testament to our enduring spirit, our unwavering resolve, and our unbreakable bond with the earth and each other. Together, we walk the path of love, truth, freedom, peace, and justice, guided by the light of the Great Law of Peace."

May this affirmation inspire and uplift, serving as a constant reminder of the powerful legacy and the bright future of Indigenous Black Autochthonous peoples, nurtured by the wisdom of the Aniyunwiya and the enduring principles of the Great Law of Peace.

We call upon the elements of the Aether, Water, Fire, Earth and Air to consume and become one with these our physical bodies (Repeat 3X)

We call upon our Ancestors for the wisdom and guidance to pursue our individual and collective purpose. To carry out that which we came to Kai, more specifically, Ta Meri – land of the Amaru-Khan, to do! (Repeat 3X)

As Mother Earth continues to cleanse and ascend and having a direct connection to her through blood and womb, we align and agree with her process, as it aligns with the Universe in consciousness, righteous retribution, redemption, and a Golden Era of the highest vibration – LOVE!

Sound Byte 2:
Amplitude

Are We There Yet?

Looking into your eyes, I wonder if you're still in love with me
It's not said as much anymore... it's not the way it used to be
Does the hurt discount all the joys and love we had?
Does the pain lead you to find an alternate rehab?

It pains my soul to realize it's not the same (damn... this shit is so lame)
No more I love you's if it's not first outta my mouth it came
Small pecks
No more tongue;
Convo's vexed
The jury's hung

I'm in a torture chamber where unsurety is master
Doubt weighing in heavy while fear falls on me faster
Gripping these heart strings and tugging the wrong direction
Has me going insane yet still grasping for lost affection

Fuck Boys

Pulled over to the side for a broken light
Told I was under the influence n just might
Go to jail for all the wrong reasons in sight...a fucked up plight!
Passed your bitch ass test, yet I'm still taking flight
Humiliation is an understatement at best
You mad or nah, that reality was addressed?
Couldn't find fault in this black man's redress
So, you issue a trumped charge to press...
I get it... I really see now
You thought it would break me and keep my head bowed
Thought I'd be another statistic of a stereotyped "in crowd"
But I held my own. Even my demeanor, for you, was too loud
If my Daddy was here, <smh>, he'd be too proud!
You couldn't break me nor instill fear with the cuffs
And that was the only way you could detain these fisticuffs.
I already called your bluff...
The hand you hold don't look too tough
I'm still gonna overstand and rise above it all!
No matter what you do or how you do it, I'll never fall!
Cuz you fail to realize even in your laws I don't recall
Any man getting locked up due to just the look in his eyeball.

Identity Crisis

I tried to be Superman
But reality soon set in
Realizing every battle I can't win
For in me lies da greatest kryptonite... being human

Constant fumbles n stumbles like Clark Kent
Tryna figure out where balance n stability went
Identity crisis is outta dis world... who am I really?
Gotta go back home n get da answers spiritually
Back to Krypton...back to Kemet...back to knowledge of originality

Birthed from da Mother, passed down thru da ancestors
A stolen legacy I need to reclaim to justify my predecessors

I tried to be Superman, so bold and bright,
But found that my struggles were an endless fight.
Reality dawned, with its lessons to teach,
That I can't always soar, can't always reach.

Every battle I faced, I couldn't always win,
I stumbled and seemed to fall into a world full of sin.
Searching for balance, for stability's grace,
In this chaotic world, in this endless race.

An identity crisis, a quest to define,
Who am I really, in this grand design?
I must journey back home, to seek what's within,
To find answers spiritually, where it all begins.

Back to Krypton, or to Kemet's embrace,

Back to the knowledge of our original place.
Born from the Mother, through ancestors' lore,
A stolen legacy, I must claim once more.

To honor those who have lit the way,
To reclaim what was lost in darkness, brought into the light of day.
I'll embrace my humanity, my strength and my flaws,
For in being true to myself, I'll find my true cause.

No longer striving for superhuman might,
I'll walk this path as me, in the day and the night.
With the wisdom of ages, in my heart and my soul,
I'll find my true purpose and make myself whole.

Just Plain Tired

Tired of feeling like a failure, like nothing will ever work
Tired of crying out of the blue, it no longer eases the
hurt
Because the pain goes deeper than these emotions
It surpasses all my doubts and uncomfortable notions
What do I have to do to make you see that we
Can make it work? Oh, we need to so desperately
Feeling all alone even though you're right by my side
The despair and hopelessness I can no longer hide
Daily struggles to pull myself up by my bootstraps
Always seem to be too low, hell, they may be trapped
The light is getting so dim on our love
Personal battles spill into nightmares I've never
dreamed of

12 Years a Slave

Twelve years a slave...
Nah, not talking about the movie they made
Nor the character which was played
But my life from 2001 up until 2013
Was anything but serene, more like a recurring soap opera scene
Intermittent parts of a bad dream
Went in with the best of intentions
But came to find out there were too many dimensions
To navigate through; losing the way on a course to ascension
Did I mention...
All the false incentives and ill-minded pretentions?
Now, don't get me wrong, it was all bad
There were some good and happy times to be had
Even if it just seemed, for the moment, to be a fad
A phase, where in turn, lessons were learned
Memories were seared, engraved, and burned
Emotions got mixed, chopped, and churned
Goals were sold for less than thirty pieces of gold
Betrayal was more valuable to you than Judas' offer of old
That stainless steel knife in the back was too cold!
And just like in the movie, all that shit wasn't supposed to happen
But the allure of self-gratification you seemed to get trapped in
And former habits before me seem to have crept back in
The chains and bondage of commitment and sacrifice
Had me bound to what I thought was the good life
Conceding to arguments where I knew I was right

Trying to repair and fix situations instead of fight
The calm, cool, collectedness of my composure
Varied greatly from your egotistical, envious, and erroneous exposure
So quick to pop off at the mouth when your ass should've been silent
So slow to believe that every reaction didn't require you to be violent.
Being your own client, you were quick to become compliant
No longer reliant
On the mental freedom you pissed away on my moral fire hydrant
Your mind... was shackled long before our vows were made
It was dimmed and covered like a light under a lamp shade
Yet, not dim enough to do something selfish and insane;
What was personal and private, you took into public domain
Emotionally whipped... demeaned and pained
I took those licks with the slightest strain
And pushed all the hurt and anguish to the back of my brain.
There, is where grew the hive
Of no longer wanting to strive
Happiness was what you wanted to deprive
Although I helped you raise and rear five,
You still continuously made the drama loud and live!
And now I'm stuck with the backlash of past trauma
PTSD, dissociation, and full-blown baby mama drama!
This CAN'T be karma!
Twelve years as a slave;

Found physical freedom, and now life has to be re-paved
Thank you, Father, I found it before the grave
Now, to go back – I've got a few more minds to save.

Embellished Trust

What do you do when there's no trust?
This hollow shell remains that we call us...
Seemingly to now always fight and fuss
Instead of rebuilding the love we share
Or showing a faint hint, showing you still care
Has withered away, seemingly no longer there
Trust being replaced by emotional thistles and thorns
Precious memories now only dreaded recaps of scorn
Not your last thought at night nor your first in the
morn
You were big on actions instead of just words
What happened to that when it came to loving me?
Seems like something I just heard...

Past Indiscretions

When I thought it was over, it was just beginning
The same kind of cycle, seems like it's never ending
I tried my best to make everything right
Not knowing the trust had been long gone from sight
Ignorant to see from the start, it was a solo fight...
smh...oh the mutha fuckin plight!!
The lie was hidden deep in the trenches
Waiting to emerge from false pretenses... covering all six senses.
The fuckery, enhanced by the fake disposition
How long did you live the lie stained by way back crimson?
You just wrote a song about how much you loved me
Lyrical tunes expressing romantic companion indemnity
You just called me and told me how you wanted to sexually enthrall me
Take it to the bedroom, promote and engage in passionate erotic tendency
But I guess that was part of the fakery
The mask finally pulled off with such dexterity
Showing the full face of young immaturity
All that went away in the blink of an eye...
Barely got a chance for the brain to apply
What the fuck just happened?! ... no reply...
Can't do it no more; thought the past was gone
In your mind it isn't, that switch is still on
Bringing vivid memories of hurt and pain
Speeding through your mind like a midnight freight train
No breaks, full speed ahead! Steady moving, but no gain
Listen...

The rest of your life is today! Marinate on that for a minute
You couldn't live life because you remained stuck in the old habit...

Hoodwinked... Bamboozled

Laying in this bed with thoughts on my mind
The reason and concluding of life I'm tryna find
Thoughts of mankind
How we've become so sublime
To the real-world issues of this day and time
Thinking it's all about what is posted on everyone's timeline
Am I the only one who sees the tie that binds?
The dumbing down of society through social media signs?
Laying in this bed, yet I'm wide awake to the elite's crimes
Of withholding true knowledge, not letting true light shine
Keeping our ears deaf, our tongues mute, and our eyes blind.

SunShine

The sun is my friend
Giving power to this melanin
Shining through to my soul within
Radiating this beautiful brown skin

Energy filled, its warmth permeates me
Refueling another day in which I'm blessed to see
Its rays stretch forth their arms openly
Embracing and molding my inner ch'i

It pierces my eyes with rejuvenation
It nurtures my pineal from its high elevation
Giving me an unending happiness... a bursting elation!

The sun is my friend; I absorb its energies
The science of it all sometimes befuddles me
Yet the spirituality of it soothes and humbles me
For where there was once darkness, now I can see

False Independence

Oh say can you see, these stars and stripes before me?
Not on that flag of our republic democracy;
But on this body...
Stars were actually scars, and stripes were just that!
Brutality – religion and country pride beaten into me
Forced to sing "My Country Tis of Thee,"
With no sign in sight of any fucking liberty!
Oh beautiful, for spacious skies...
Hmmmph! The lies!!
Cuz contrary to popular belief,
These skies only gave me limits and grief!
Kept me stuck in an 8x10 like Kalief
But you say I shouldn't hold no beef?
How, Sway? You just expect me to forgive and pray?
To believe that a savior you introduced me to, will
somehow make a way?!
Nah, not when your foundation is made from clay
See, I KNOW my roots and ancestors were set in stone
A permanence you can't shake from these bones
These generational and cultural skills you can NEVER
hone
So all the fear you try to instill... all the tears you make
me cry
Will never feel as good to you, than me shouting with
raised fist,
FUCK YOUR 4th OF JULY!

Not What It Seems

Beware of what lurks beneath!
To AmeriKKKA, our faith we bequeath
On the surface, it all looks patriotic;
Little did they tell you about how chaotic
That undertow can be if you don't pay attention
And get sucked under... and maybe die without mention
Wear that flag proudly
Or shout for liberty loudly...
No one really gives a shit how devoutly
You stand by your country
Because in the end, she'll only betray
And possibly slay
Any liberties you thought came your way
Then smile that evil, twisted smile and say,
"Have a nice day!"
So, ride the wave of opportunity cautiously
Or else become shark bait in that grand sea odyssey

The Way, The Truth, The Light

Never have I ever
Seen the free willed, so willfully ignorant
Much like a dramatic sever;
Or an immediate and blatant recant
Knowledge had been cast by the wayside...

When it was a hidden jewel,
Many sought after it at a mortal cost.
Only after Greeks began to rule,
Did it begin to get burned or "lost."
Knowledge became an evading thought...

That gnosis, that Aletheia, that truth
Into the wrong hands breeds corruption
The wondrous wealth of the sayer sooth
Now an overspill and vast eruption.
Knowledge became available once again...

They fucked around and gave us the Net
And now we have unlimited sourcing;
Slowly unlocking the keys and secrets
Freedom by Truth and Light enforcing
Knowledge is the biggest problem now...

E – An Alliteration

Excitedly and eagerly awaiting this exit
Education graduation, from college... bless it!
Expounding exponentially in electronics
Earth shattering grades I made – tectonic!

Ever evolving into something greater
Each step exudes efficient efforts
Exclaiming eccentric "Fuck you's" to every hater
Erasing and eradicating their retorts.

I'm embracing all emerging epithets,
Positive energy, and ecclesiastical exclamations
Congratulatory gestures and exuberant exhortations
More enigmatic elations than the POTUS gets!

Excuse my extra excitement, but it's been a long road
An elongated, elevated, and treacherous goad.
Yet, I've now expeditiously expunged that load!

End piece.

Poet's Delight

Rippin' and runnin' through words on this page
Rapidly firing shots of ink on this literary stage
Our rhetoric relays a redeeming peace;
Emotional rollercoasters becoming our thrill of release
Rewriting and editing lines of ill and dope rhyme
A better conglomeration than Rawkus Records in their prime
We rock what's right when we write or speak
Relaying issues, concerns, or even comedy peaks
Grammar and etymology stay in constant tweak
Relevance never dies... we get multiple redo's and tries
Our words replacing laughter, shock, hurt, or cries
Whether we roll with the tide
Or run ravenously with the pride,
Our words on paper will be something you can NEVER hide!

The Question Is...

Fellas – when we gone learn? Huh?
When will we finally make that right turn?
And face what's clearly evident in history;
The obvious no long being a mystery
Thinking logically and critically,
Instead of chauvinistically
You would not be here had it not been for a woman!
Had she not had the strength to laboriously summon
All her power to form, nourish, and PUSH you into existence from within
Give you the breath of life as well as supple sustenance!
For that very reason, you should worship the earth she has trodden;
Her gifts to this world should never be discounted nor forgotten
Check my diction...
When will you stop being a dick,
And learn to be an addiction?
Curb that letter 'c' and become an addition?
That Yang to her Yin, instead of calculated attrition?

Ladies – ohhhhh ladies! Has it really come down to this?
Settling for the unqualified and disconnected imitation apprentice?
To think that you're really doing something via viral videos –
Only attracting the sneaky link, good for nothing, passport "bros."
Or considering to be a stud, when in fact, you're still an undercover ho.
Pardon my rhetoric, but we really need to explore this

The psychological parameters of this attention whore bliss.
There are still wonderful men out there seeking;
Awaiting your Goddess activation to start piquing!
Patience is a virtue... but so are standards and morals
Be true to yourself, first, instead of to others where you find quarrels
And if your preference is to not mingle and stay single,
Then continue to let your light shine big and twinkle!
You're worth far more than your weight in gold...
And this comes from a place of Love what you're being told
Never discount yourself nor fold
To the wiles of society where everything can be sold!
In the end, it all boils down to the pedestal you choose to uphold.

End Game

They're trying to spread out and disperse our Queens,
While simultaneously trying to stack out Kings
Separation of church (male) and state (female) by any means
Not through natural, but by way of diabolical things

And you STILL have yet to see
How the wool covers your eyes so comfortably
Whether it's race, politics, religion, or sexuality
These are all surface issues that lead you blindly
Wake up and realize your most powerful weapon is Family!

The unit that seals, binds, and combines;
Where loyalty lurks, and true love shines!
But that's why they'll win every single time;
Cuz your incohesive ass runnin' that "independent" line!

The last drop of crazy glue that we had
Was washed away in the 60's by trending fads
Their agendas we adopted; and made us feel adopted, accepted, and glad
Our armor finally reduced to aluminum after being ironclad

And in the meanwhile, your ignorant ass is over here playing checkers
Going for the single punch while they hand out double deckers!
Yelling out, "King me!" Or performing elaborate jumps...

As they strategize and make precision moves through financial or economic bumps
All the while, whispering, "Checkmate..."

For example, you get a record deal... that's a "King me"
While they own the record label and the masters... that's a "Checkmate"

You make it to the pros... that's a "King me"
They're out here buying/owning the franchise... that's a "Checkmate"

You march for freedom and equality... that's a "King me"
They kill Malcolm and Martin... that's a "Checkmate"

Do you realize how the tables would turn,
If we came together as FAMILY, and rose as water in an overflowing cistern?
The pressure alone would be enough to churn
Corruption and propaganda into laid waste that deliberately burns!

But first we must rebuild, reconnect, and reconcile with each other...
The black child, the black father, the black mother
All becoming one in strong solidarity and unity
Then taking that and spreading it throughout each community!

You know we make anything we touch, GREAT!

Just here alone, for over 400 years they've tried to seal our fate
Only for their plans to backfire;
And their evil intentions to dissipate!

We don't need their idea of restitution;
Nor do we care for their theories of redistribution
We have our own solution
As well as our own empowered retribution!

As long as we continue to live and fight for what's right;
At any given height of racial, political, or religious spite...
We should still be shouting Kendrick's words,
"WE gone be alright!"

All Eyez on Me
(The Woes and Backfiring of Social Media)

I captured my beauty and thought it was just for you
Afraid to open up in the beginning, slowly gaining trust's view.
You played the part so well... I just couldn't tell
Of the betrayal you'd introduce me to... last name, Hell.

I only had eyes for you; didn't know you were a salesman.
Selling my pics online for a Judas price gonna have me needing a bail man.
Now the world can see me in all my bare glory;
How can I ever live down this headline story?

Intimate selfies, I thought they were
Turned into a nightmare I couldn't concur.
How I wish those pics came to your phone in a blur.
Shit! Beauty, what kind of fuckin mess did you stir?

I feel like the whole world is laughing at me
All because on one night, I was feeling a little frisky.
Because I wanted to share something with you in privacy;
I sarcastically, and with enmity, thank you for ruining my life socially and publicly.

What a Life – Just Unjust

The black life is just a setup
Planned by those who've already surpassed the come up;
Easily deceived because we won't wake up
But rather shake up (party) and bake up (get high)!
Just ran across a video yesterday;
And I did press play
A white woman going through hell,
Shown the utmost mercy and justice – free bail
Pity was the verdict in this tale
And I wondered, would she have been shown that kinda slack,
Had her skin tone been black?
Hell no! Not even the slightest crack!
It angers me to see that to this end,
We still can't comprehend by justice we can't befriend
'Cause in AmeriKKKa, justice is just pretend
And will never defend
Our natural born rights that we steadily try to amend
And for that, it shouldn't even matter what laws we break or bend;
Because they were never for us to obey, or even contend.

Before the 3rd Awakening

Trump ain't my President!
And I no longer consider myself a resident
Of a country ruled by a Twitter king;
Who fashions global policy around a social media ring!
Shit is more like a media circus
Where tabloids are quick to splurge this
Number 45 looking like an ad for Sunkist
Bursting with orange flavor, but not really missed
Only in AmeriKKKa can you find a clown
To lead a nation below the depths you could drown
This It looking mother fucker brings on strictly frowns
Yet have I to see any positive actions...
Questioning his deeds like Janet Jackson;
What have you done for me lately?
Nothing... I mean NOTHING has been done stately!
Diplomatic what?! More like
DIP-LOW-AUTOMATICALLY!
Ducking and dodging these racist bullets dramatically
Listen! Because I'm speaking emphatically!
Questions aren't asked rhetorically;
When will you wake up?
Why must our culture continually get raked up?
What are you doing to prevent the gentrified shake up?
How can you be blinded by the powder puff clouds?
Makeup!
Concealment at its very best, where we refuse to address
Hidden truths that originally put us in this mess
Being comfortable with lies that we still stroke and caress
With the gift of gab that you like to call a finesse...
But... (sigh)... I digress...

Play No More

I had to push pause on my passion for a bit;
Had to hold my tongue from lashing out and shit
Play this game of chess
Steer clear of judicial mess
Don't need that extra stress
Inhale... exhale... nevertheless
Tired of playing nice when I could easily slice
Into pieces, your world. But at what price?
To me, my children are more than just a child support check
I give them more than the material aspects you expect!
A nurturing love has no dollar amount
The many times I've sat and listened, you couldn't even count!
Your brazen Brooklyn shout(ing); what the hell is that all about?
I'm no subject matter expert in raising kids,
But I do have the wisdom to follow what many others did
Not casting hollow bids, betting on tomorrow's biz
An unsure date
Will ultimately seal your fate
Of what you wished for my future, you should've acted on in the "NOW" state.
Now it's too late...
No need to think on your next move...
I've already called CHECKMATE!

Enveloped Pain

Being hurt
Not even realizing the extent...
Anger pain and frustration never the intent
Although it wasn't meant,
Still left a huge dent... and ostensible scent
Realization now becomes baffled wonderment
No longer content
Hopes and dreams are spent
Used to be priceless...
Now not worth one red cent
Path of trust and love now forever bent
And the damage done, I heavily lament
Being hurt

FREESTYLE

They say study to show yourself approved;
But the pages never moved
And curiosity was never soothed
Ignorance was indeed, bliss...
Knowledge became remiss;
Slithering by to the sound of a serpent's hiss.
Rolling by in numerous books other than the Bible.
Surely, by now, you MUST know there are more golden nuggets necessary for survival!
Faith has become somewhat tribal;
And thru that, you become libel
And susceptible to fairy tales as truth.
Meanwhile, your mind is steadily aloof
Because you refuse to see the proof!
And my people perish from the lack thereof...
Afraid to take care of...
Or rather take cover from deceptive tactics towards our natural spirituality.
How long shall we keep our souls in torturous melee?
It's definitely time to rewrite the story.
But, what's the point if we can't pick up a book other than what they deem is "holy?"

Issa Rap (Wrap)

One, two... one, two... the count is on
Mic check... mic check... is this thing on?
I'm in need of your attention...
Cuz I'm about to mention
Some etymologic repass to get past this 3rd dimension.
One question I must first ask you -
DO YOU KNOW HOW GREAT YOU ARE?!
It damn sure ain't no coincidence, by far!
You are evolution from that Sirius star!
You are revolution of the Ancestors' scar!
The time of restoration and recompense is now!
Look and feel around you; realize how
The energy has indeed shifted in our favor;
You just have to know how to handle it and savor
The universal and cosmic karma that comes to save her (Earth).
You are a hueman processing unit - digital
Downloading ancestral and akashic memory - pivotal
Gathering data that's direct but also subliminal
Maximal storage capacity - never the minimal
The matrix will have you stayin in a constant state of defeat;
Still babies nibbling on crumbs and milk while I'm devouring the meat
Knowledge, that is... that substance and sustainer
The everlasting retainer
Need a larger container so I can contain her
On my Goku shit... fireballs I spit
Tryna reach ya cerebellum
Somebody needs to tell em
How to rage against the machine

To be heard as well as seen
Slickin ya wigs back with vibratory oil sheen
Injections into your medulla oblongata
This hypodermic vial is bound to be hotter;
More addictive than crack cocaine
Yet the side effects won't make you insane
But instead, will make you train
The mind to think differently... more so, critically
Clear the static, cuz we're doing this dynamically!
Our life force never dies; that's eternal inner ch'i
Waiting to explode and expound this wisdom like nuclear energy
Shit's got to be planned systematically
And carried out emphatically
Cuz if not, we're damned to repeat this holographic cycle more dramatically
WAKE YA ASSES UP!!

Retrieving the Spoils of War

A desolate and dark world in which we live!
Where is the light that you promised to give?
Walkin' around amongst so many unconscious minds;
Tryin' to break loose from the heavy tie that binds.

Freedom of speech, press, religion...all gone out the window!
You say I have unalienable rights...but do I really, though?
I see my 1st amendment off in the far and cold distance!
Taunting and teasing ------ hypnotizing me into a trance.

Leaders bought off and bribed...sold out to a New World's Orders!
Paid to bring Nazis over, turned the other cheek to open our borders!
When will we wake up, see the error of our ways, and FIGHT?!
When will we discover the TRUTH? And go back to what's right

Fully ours? A country run by the people! One nation under God.
Wake up, zombies and robots! Walk the new path we've trod.
Like Public Enemy said, "We gotta fight the powers that be!"
Bring back the two most important spoils we've lost...LOVE N LIBERTY!

Alliterated Thoughts

Thoughts
Tangible Touches
One Track Mind
Or Two-Way Street
Tinkering Time Bombs Ticking Away
Tools for Training and Torquing Life
Timid or Terrible Transitions Becoming Transactions
Tick... Tock... Turning the Tremendous
Travel Clock of Time
Toiling Through Temporary Decisions
Taking Teeter Tottered Steps
Tweaking the Tendrils of This Brain
Thoughts

Autochthonous

Of ancient lands and skies they sing,
Autochthonous beings, born with a wing.
Connected to soil, roots in the earth,
Stories and wisdom, of infinite worth.

From time's deepest well, they arise,
In harmony with nature, under open skies.
Guardians of lands, a mystical sight,
Autochthonous beings, bathed in light.

Their tales woven in rivers and trees,
Whispering secrets in every breeze.
With heritage deep, their spirits entwine,
Autochthonous beings, guardians of time.

In unity with nature, they dance and sway,
Preserving traditions, come what may.
A tribute to them, this humble rhyme,
Autochthonous beings, beyond space and time.

Sound Byte 3:
Crescendo/Climax

Random Thoughts

Your wet pussy calls me with its purr
Beckoning to my manhood to rise and incur
An excitement only you can give me
Patterned breath from repetitious melee
Climaxing together in unified screams
Still making love afterwards in each other's dreams
Love sessions in spurts of bliss
Souls connected from a single kiss
You really have no clue what you do to me
Just to gaze upon you makes my heart beat incessantly
Got me open, but I'm not tripping
Cuz when I spread those legs, your fountain starts dripping
Drip, drop... drip drippity drop
All roads lead to "GO"...ain't no way you want me to stop
Your body I'll browse as well as shop

Cosmically Grounded Kiss

Our embrace exudes a quantum entanglement glow

As above, so below is the energetic flow

Wrapped in each other's heavenly and earthen elements

Suspended and encased in our NOW, where time has no relevance

My watery galaxy floods your lush and luminous celestial cluster

The touch of our lips together is far above lackluster!

Natural and magnetic bonding electrifies our feminine and masculine poles

Shifting a raging QuietStorm and Sweetness into balanced, placated roles.

As we become One with the Universe, we are expressed in many facets

Combining forces to create ethereal, cosmic classics

To think, these magical moments emblazoned in bliss

Began from one cosmically grounded kiss...

Prelude to Erotica

Rose petals in your bath water...candles by your bedside
Your soft caramel silhouette in da doorway proving
there's nothing to hide
Tonight's da night where the art of love, lust, n sex
Becomes our masterpiece of a mind blowing complex
Where your pussy drips n hinges on every word
whispered in your ear
Your wetness glazes my face and your ass smothers me
as I pull u near
No no no Baby, this is not just an ordinary fuck session
This is school time, where you the student come to learn
your lesson
As we explore each other's blessing;
Pleasures and desires we're undressing
All acts of seductive sensuality we're testing
I can tell that on you and in you, I've found something
new...
Your deep heavy breathing and guttural moans give me
that clue
And from there we elude to the highest form of
eroticism.
Tranquil yet turbulent... tender yet ravaging...
And you will know on this night of sex scavenging
I came to erode your mind with elicit thoughts of love
making
Dat grind hard, deep stroke, eye roll, back breaking
Nail digging, clit throbbing, lip biting, body shaking
Type of loving where the aftershocks are just as

amazing as the bodyquaking
And I haven't even put it in yet... that's just a prelude...

Fight for Your Love

I'll tell you I love you every single day
I'll continue to kiss your lips even if you say
That you no longer want... no longer need it
Cause in the end it will be worth every bit

I know you're mad, I know you still hurt inside
But let's cut all of the bullshit and push away any pride
Put our love back into action, full overdrive
That's the only way we will ever survive
Taking it full throttle one day at a time

Starting a healing process together
Back to basics of dating and just enjoying each other
Moving in the direction we started... friends before lovers
Back to what Chris Brown said, start to "Discover"

I'll tell you I love every single day
Continue to reach for hugs in spite of your dismay
I'll keep reaching for "us" as long as it takes
Hoping this union, this bond, never breaks

Knowing it takes more than just these words
Things will take time to be seen, not just heard
The time having to be put in with a sense of urge
Emotions of doubt and fear needing to be purged

Finding out faith again is the first big step
Building each other on a spiritual level, in depth
First becoming one with our Creator, then one again in each other

Connecting mentally and emotionally… then physically… friends before lovers

Missing You

I miss your deep kisses and your soft touch
I miss moments when sleep wasn't too much
When you held me back, hands over mine and such
Shifting your sexy caramel body towards me like a five-speed clutch

I miss spinning your record player...
Your clit grinding my fingertips
Hearing you climax in layer upon layer
Moans intensified by deep scratches and grips

I miss your breath on my lips, your drool on my chest
Lost in emotional bliss as we tried our best to rest
Just simply laying in the dark in complete content
Losing all track of time, not knowing or caring where it went

I miss being the very first thing on your mind
The reasons for an awaiting text you never had to find
I miss the thought of being number one in your life
I miss you altogether... guess I miss me too... because you are my life.

Self-Love's Ballad

One of a kind to me you are
A deep and buried treasure from lands afar
Traveled through life seeking and searching for your heart
On a mission for unconditional love, a bond that never parts
No matter what we go through, no matter what's said
I'll love you until the day I transition, from alive to dead
Wipe your tears and wash your pain away instead
Guiding you to the light of true fulfillment ahead
In time, all things will come to pass
Every heart's desire and good thought it has
Memories that will forever be tucked away to last
Life and its beauty begin today inside you
Both have been with you all along, you just had no clue
Time to connect the dots and mend the brokenness with the glue
That seals an eternal commitment of what has been tried and true
Committed to loving self in all of its shapes and forms
Knowing your divine uniqueness has never ever been the norm
Open your eyes and see your true beauty before it's too late
And know from day one, it has always been one life... one love... CHECKMATE!!

Black Gold (Not Oil)

I am the true black gold! My disposition
Brings about fiery-fueled opposition!
Oiled and coiled, but I'm not slick;
Regal curves, voluptuous bust, and bootylicious thick.
Illumination... I shine - everywhere I go, I flow

The sun, being my crowning jewel,
Adoration come from the renown;
While the earth I have as my footstool,
The Universe ensures to hold a Sista down!

The epitome of Beauty -
Splendid attraction

The embodiment of Love -
Complete satisfaction

The poise of Grace -
Humanity's salvation

The humbleness of Divinity -
Ancestral oblations

I am the pinnacle of creation!
The Creator's greatest ideation!
Brainpower like Lucy!
All four lips stay full and juicy...

Once we come into contact,
You can never loose me
Forever embedded like foundations,

I began it all... the mother of ALL nations!

Unification

When the horizontal heavens meet the rushing earthly seas
Our souls, to the Universe, doth greatly appease
As above, so let it be below
Majestic unification in our aura and glow
Intertwined into the vines of eternity,
Two different worlds combined for longevity
Carpe diem! For the morrow is not promised!
To the here and now, we bask in its ambiance
And pay homage
To the everlasting and glorious Medu Neter;
The Supreme energy of him and her
All blessings we do incur
And all negativity we do deter!
The atmosphere is ours and what we have in common
Ever grateful for the gifts of the Amen (Ra).

Indulgent Nikki (Ode to Prince)

Hi, my name is Nikki, and I'm a fiend.
I desire and crave the thrills of life –
If you know what I mean.
Met this guy name Prince a while back;
He was dressed in purple and black
Even put me on a track.
See, I bought this toy to match his fly
Riding together, passing Lake Minnetonka on by.
Arrived instead at Devil's Cliff
Stood on the horizon's drift;
Then plunged over, free falling into a bungee shift
What a fucking rush!
Diving into the plush
Winds that were beneath our wings
Entrusting life to rubberized, elastic strings!
He is my Purple Rain, and I'm his Orange Sunrise
We appease and fulfill each other through our Dove
Cries.

Magnetism

As I draw closer to you, do you feel that energy?
Mmmmmm... that's that synergy!
Syncopation in thoughts and action;
Forget fatal, this is wholistic attraction!
Ever brewing, ever growing...
Ever learning, ever knowing
Soon, we'll be ready; feel the steam rising?
Able to withstand stormy seas with no capsizing
Only capitalizing
No more ostracizing
But only compromising through empathizing
Two is always better than one;
But when one is made from two... to me, that's
completion!

Illusions of Grandeur

Tropical...
Erotica exotica
Sun-kissed and earth fed
Warm, inviting, delighting, hypnotizing
Mesmerizing
Temperatures rising
Arcing like a rainbow,
I do glow
Got that Crayola 64 flow
Accenting green acres
Give pause to all movers and shakers
The real deal... no family dollar fakers
Flower power!
Set to bloom at any given hour
Out of darkness came light...
No shade
Au naturale, not man made

Workout

My milk does her body real good
Strengthens and fortifies like vitamin D should
I'd give her more nutrition if I could;
Be her daily supplement, in hourly increments, I would.

I'm her protein shake... I fill her up and give her that boost
Always more than one scoop, I try to stick with the deuce
But she craves my energy; and I willingly share
Her appetite is voracious; of that she's made me aware

I'm her personal trainer... keeping her weekly schedule intact.
Charting her progress and documenting the resultant facts.
Like a long-distance runner, I keep her on track;
Through cardio, Kama sutra, or blowing out her back!

Getting Served

I got my fork, knife, and spoon... and I'm ready to dine!
Baby, scoot up on this table and lemme drink from the Divine Vine!
While I'm lickin' and sippin'
And you're steady drippin'
I catch each drop 'cuz Momma always said,
"Don't let good food go to waste... you trippin'!!"
You cater to me like Destiny's Child
But I'm more like Khaled and Rihanna – thoughts are WILD!
I could make love to you like Boyz II Men;
Or put it in ya muthafuckin' mouth... an Akinyele sin!
Turn you around and give them long deep strokes
Or we can serve each other a 69 menu and make each other choke!
Put your nipple in my mouth; it's like the cherry on top
And those two scoops in my hands –
Well, four, because first the breasts and then the ass –
Are like ice cream scoops, and I eat every damn drop!
Slide up and down on me... honey glaze this magic stick
Now, close your eyes and open your mouth;
Because dessert will be the best magic trick!

Imprints in Black Paradise

Kissing you under moonlit skies
Tongue waves crashing between your thighs
Intimate hugs, ecstasy highs
Imprints in the sand where your body lies
Passion exploding on the vast beaches
Moans being heard as far as sound reaches
Lessons being learned that body language teaches
Holding on to each other like parasitic leeches...
She said I give her goosebumps
And make her kitty purr;
I told her she gives me butterflies,
A fluttering I never want to deter
We looked into each other's pretty brown eyes
Deeply searching our mint conditioned souls for lies
Yet, we found none, only opened minds and hearts that try
Explosive love that sends chills and shivers
Repetitive orgasms that flood like rivers
Blowing backs out like pulled triggers
Withdrawals and deposits in our personal accounts – Still 7 figures
And it's not just the lovin' that appeases us
Laughter, ease of comfort, and general convo pleases us
Nuts aren't the only things we tend to bust;
And our lower extremities aren't the only parts we can trust.
Yes, my heart replies with fluttering cries
Of peaceful serenity that lies
In the sunset we share with a hopeful gaze
A toast to the good life with glasses raised
And maybe even the purple haze

Will make us forget about all the craze
We left behind while tryna find
Golden brown sands
Where we could bury our hands
As well as our minds in never never land
But this ain't no damned Peter Pan!
Shores of crystal blue
Permeate our varied brown hues
And just for a moment, we're lost without a clue
Lost in each other and not wanting to find
A different space, different place, or time
Cuz paradise is in both our eyes, and we call it sunshine!

AN EXCITATION DECLARATION

The purpose of this notice is to inform all parties, known and unknown, and specifically to all tribes of the Americas (North, Central, and South) that the United States corporate entity, known as the United States or United States, Inc. is dead and over with! The Vatican control of the Earth is no more! The city-state governmental reign of Rome, London, and Washington D.C. has met its demise!

Understand that we, the Originals of Turtle Island - the Ongwehonweh - individually known as North America, Central America, and South America - have been in a conjure war for the past 500+ years. As of July 6, 2019, that conjure was broken; and under the continuity of government and specific executive orders, we are returning to a rightful order of law of the land versus the maritime/admiralty/salvage laws we have been oppressed under for so long. However, if you do not understand the different types of law nor understand your sovereign status as a true, living entity vs. operating as a strawman or dead entity (corpse), then you will not be able to grasp what is being said here.

The Matriarchal form of government, in accordance with and under the Great Law, the Continuity of Government through FEMA, United Nations Declaration of Rights of Indigenous Peoples (UNDRIP), and the Declaration of American Indigenous Rights (DecAmIn), is now in the process of being restored.

We are seeking due recourse in the expression and expansion of Matriarchal systems, with proper and just restitution, reallocation, and restoration of all land and resources that were stolen and abused by the United States corporation since 1492 A.D.

The truth is that someone lied to your great grandparents, who in turn, lied to your grandparents. Your grandparents then lied to your parents; and your parents lied to you! Although it may not have been intentional, it doesn't change to fact that it was done to keep you from ever knowing who you really are! Indigenous, Indian, tribal, African-American, black, colored, or any other exonym, classification, and/or misnomer no longer suffices to be considered our identity. A good number of us, who know no other homeland, are indeed ORIGINAL and ORGANIC to this land!!

What has happened to us – and what confuses us – is that different, home-grown tribes have been led to believe that those who look like us, but aren't us, derived an identity system of classification to place us under. That system, which was created by black Europeans, labeled, and enforced a caste method that was predicated upon a doctrine we've come to know as white supremacy. Said doctrine was then brought over here to the Americas specifically as a war strategy and we were ultimately held in reprisal for a debt that we never owed.

In understanding the Matriarchal form of government, we must realize that it is now and has been in full effect, even though we may not see it due to still present patriarchal factors and promoters – explicitly, the mainstream media. The purpose of the Matriarchy is to be of service TO the people, regardless of race, color, creed, philosophical background, or destructive religious doctrines. That is not to say that you can't hold on to whatever it is that you believe, because at the end of the day, we all exercise a free will. However, a belief will not sustain the inherent Truth; and that Truth is not always pretty or what we know as good. Matriarchy acts in the Spirit of Truth, unlike Patriarchy, which acts in abusive power and physicality or many falsehoods.

We are calling forth any and all clan or tribal mothers that understand and know who they and their ancestors are; that they step forth to claim the birthright and inheritance of the original and organic people of this land! Your HERitage is far more important and valid than HIStory!

As a representative of the Divine Masculine, in service to the Great Mother and guardian/defender/protector of the Divine Feminine, this is a call, or proclamation to all Wombmen – sisters, daughters, mothers, and grandmothers – to join together in a great return of the Ancient Ones so that we can reclaim what is rightfully ours by blood rite and by birthright. To show through works and deeds that we are more than capable of sustaining ourselves in all aspects –

politically, socially, economically, health wise, educationally, and geographically.

Our children are the overall goal of the Matriarchy - to not allow them to be indoctrinated or trained to be just laborers. But to go through natural tribal rites of passage education where they are allowed to choose their own life path, and we as parents give them the necessary tools required to construct a future for themselves according to their character, personality dictate... not how we want them to be!

Under the Matriarchy, we are no longer bound by the Columbian era (1492-2019) treaties, contracts, legalese, or artificial paperwork that they used to usurp our jurisdictional supremacy as the caregivers of the land. We no longer acknowledge ANY of their corporate/legal fiction; and through usage of the continuity of government program, we will be made aware of actual events so that the collective can act in real time without the confusion of the media, CIA, or other nefarious forces that seek to keep us enslaved.

Sound Byte 4 –
Transformation

Power to Our People!

They stole our land, they broke up our tribes
Gave us weapons of destruction loaded with false incentives and bribes
Stolen legacies... brutal rapes... plagiarism of our heritage
A deafening and permanent silence you tried to instill in our lineage
But we can't we silenced! We can't be defeated!
Our ancestors' blood fuels our souls and shouts, "WE WILL NOT BE DELETED!"
From Tamir Rice to Emmett Till... to MLK and Malcolm X,
From Kunta to Shaka, our memories of them are our natural Celebrex
Their written words can't hide nor cover what's engraved in stone!
Our power emanates from within! Melanated Kings and Queens from a totally different time zone...
Righteousness endows us! Wisdom bestows us!
Knowledge and Understanding subdues us!
And yet... they think it's in their god that we trust?
Sadly mistaken my depigmented brutha...
For when it comes to spirituality, we'll choose the other
The lessons of consciousness and of the third eye,
The golden rule, as well as the laws and confessions of Ma'at we apply
Score is 42 to 10... what? No reply?
A systematic educating of not just the mind, but the souls of black folk
Keeping in line with what our Creator, our Supreme Energy allows us to invoke.
Regal and distinguished living with a sense of pride

Our displaced royalty we must recover in stride
Not allowing their false intimidation and lies to have us cower!
OUR history! OUR antiquated stories and beliefs, on OUR children, we must shower.

And once they believe it, learn it, know it - Haaaaa! B... L... K?? Now that's BLK POWER!

Lose My Mind

I gotta be honest, I'm losing my mind yet still tryna find it
Lost in the maze of hurt, anger, n pain
Tryna recover da good dats been gained
I lose sleep thinkin of all da wrong dats been done
But I need to lose this mind and find me a new one

Losing my mind, I'm just losing my mind
New patterned thoughts I need to find
Stop hittin the pause, stop pressing rewind
Cause if I don't, I'll just keep being blind

Lose my mind... or continue being blind
It's time to refocus, gotta start building from what lies inside

Starting with trust, then love then laughter
Sharing our vibes of happily ever after
In the depths of despair, where emotions entwine,
I'm struggling to find what was once truly mine,

Lost in a maze of hurt, anger, and pain,
Searching for sunshine through the endless rain.

I lose sleep at night, haunted by my past,
Every regret and mistake, they're all here to last,
But I've realized now, it's time for a change,
To lose my old mind and rearrange.

Losing my mind, I've decided to embrace,
New patterns of thought, a different kind of space,
No more pressing rewind, no more looking behind,
It's time to let go and free my heart and mind.

Lose my mind or continue being blind,
The choice is before me, and it's time to unwind,
To refocus my energy, to build from within,
Starting with trust, letting love gently begin.

With laughter and joy, I'll rewrite my story,
Sharing vibes of happiness, of unbound glory,
It's time for a journey, a beautiful quest,
To rediscover myself and be at my very best.

Sinner Man

Sinners have a soul, too!
I falter, I fail, I do wrong as other's do
Is God trying to tell me something?
Am I ready to listen? That's the real question.
Maybe it's not that the sinner has soul,
But that the soul is capable of sin... huge difference.
According to your New Testament, the latter makes more sense.
My ears and eyes are open to good AND evil...
Ultimately, it's up to me to choose the path
That which is lawful, or what may be lethal.
It is said, "When I would do good, evil is always present..."
And this right here is the true lesson;
The balance of it all becomes the real blessing
Sinners have a soul... but the soul doesn't have to sin
In fact, it can WIN WIN WIN!
Triumph over transgression
With precise discretion...
A ballot in whose election
I choose to vote for and make the righteous selection
So speak Lawd... speak to me
'Cause my heart and mind are the locks;
And Your voice is the key

Lingering Spirit

There have been heavy signs of your presence these past few weeks,
Mind is wandering and wondering as to of what this speaks
I know you're with me wherever I go
Your spirit envelopes me as I keep pushing to and fro
The older I get, the more I favor your countenance
A few have said that they see you in me, in more abundance
And I'm coming to terms with their stance
Looking like the both of you at first glance
Haven't really grieved for you since you've left
The pain still seems to be a dream so surreal
But it's only one sixteenth of how Mummy feels...
Continue resting in peace; no tears in heaven, no crying in glory
Keep your spirit near me daily, guide me as I write my life's story.

I love you Daddy-O!

Maybe One Day

May one day we'll get off our ass
And realize we come from a distinguished class
Instead of trash, or a system polluted by caste
Maybe one day we'll rise into our hereditary greatness
Like a tree planted with deep roots in the land we call blessed
Africa, Alkebulan, Kemet, Nigeria, Liberia, Sierra Leone
Lands of Kings and Queens who ruled from a true throne
Filled with riches and knowledge that every inhabitant could own
Yeah, maybe one day...
Maybe one day we'll exemplify our true power
Instead of behind protests or legislation which we cower
And literally fight for our rights, with a knowledge storm to shower
Impeding a system that never care about our welfare
Yet our culture and diversity they'll exploit and share
Maybe one day, the Lion Kings/Queens from Pride Rock will return...
But until that day, if revolution doesn't occur, we'll continue to be stampeded and burned!
TIME TO RISE!!

Grief (2016)

It's been four years and I finally get to address
The pain, the anger, the grief, the stress
Heart is aching like it just happened
Seems like yesterday we were just on that park bench rappin
I looked into your eyes and I saw the despair
Yet, I still saw your hope and faith in that stare
Wanted to ease your pain and dis-ease
Praying to God to quickly seize
Whatever was attacking your body, it needed to leave
Memories flood my head like they do on people's timelines
So many time times I've wished I was there before they pulled your lifeline
You enjoyed on last Christmas at my house and I wasn't even there
Across that water providing for a family who didn't even care
Nor understood the heavy burden I would soon bear
The heartache is real, the loneliness too deep
Just thinking about you speaking or singing makes me weep
Been trying to be strong and provide like you always taught
But the shoulder's weight is heavy and the battles' still being fought
To regain the balance I one had before being knocked
Life seemed to throw a sucker punch; mind really got rocked!
Now I'm trying to pick up the pieces and put it all back together
This storm blew a big piece of me away... I'm weathered.

At least now I can express these feelings in this process
And begin to clean and scrub this mental and emotional mess
I am now the personification of long-term grief
Yet through it all, it shall not shatter my foundational beliefs
The aftermath is always worse than the actual storm
Accessing the damage, cost, and totality of what is no longer the norm
Grieving on so many levels where all seems lost and in a jumble
But I'm still pressing towards a mark in which I cannot fumble
You're the one who taught me to never give up
To always look towards the hills... to look up
And now I look up more than ever to the clouds and skies
For now, that's where a portion of my Creator resides.

Alarm Clock

I woke up to a wake up, mind blown because of the shake up
To a reality, where my eyes finally
Realized that most shit was just a make up
Bible tales being true allegories
History just the white man's stories
Shunning and erasing the Black King's glories
Contributions to life and liberty denied
Our spirituality and ancestry he tried to hide
By taking away our culture, our names
Replacing them with the edicts of a beast they called King James
An usurper of a throne we inherently owned
Back in the Motherland filled w/riches and colored stones

Wake up! Time to stand and not stagger
Need to focus on the Negus or the Naga
Reclaiming a royalty that we can brag of!

Yes! RECLAIM! Meaning something we once were
For at one time it was to us they brought the gold, frankincense, and myrrh

Stop being plain and ordinary niggas!
The picture, the cause is so much bigga!
But you can't see clear when your pineal shows fluoridated and clouded figures

En Vogue said it best: "Free your mind, and the rest will follow..."
Know that the weapon inside your head is not an empty mass or sleepy hollow

Build it and fight with it for today! Because truth be
told,
No one knows if there will be a tomorrow.

The Fight of Your Life

Believe it or not, everyone goes through this.
We try so hard to throw back punches… and mostly miss
Objectively, life is just a heavyweight contender
And we train daily to defend her
Never the pretender
But ALWAYS an offenser!
We fight… and fight… and fight some more
But the one thing we can never ignore
Is the HOPE to correctly restore
Our hearts and minds right at our front door
To come out of that corner better than before
And retrieve that prize of second chances galore!
You're worth fighting for! Let no one tell you different
Because your purpose and personality were all meant
To shape you in YOU; and in doing so, to be confident
That this season shall soon wither and pass…
And yes, things may tend to clash
Just remember you have someone in your corner always –
Your personal and secret stash.
It's ultimately up to you to go pound for pound;
And the victory is only made sweeter when that support group is around
How does that sound?
The bell tolling for new life being found
Hmmmph! And you thought you were down?!
Nope! You just had to shake the dust off and adjust your crown.
We do royal things over here;
So go ahead – speak that shit into your atmosphere
And make it perfectly clear,

That you hold life's reins, and it's your destiny that you steer.

K.R.S. One (Knowledge Reigns Supreme over One)

They say knowledge reigns supreme;
And it does, in the correct aspect of things.
Yet, one thing knowledge bows to, it seems,
Is death, and its gaping hole lingerings.

One thing that eludes knowledge, is time.
Not knowing when that life clock will suddenly stop
Unbeknownst to anyone when they'll just drop
Mourning loved ones... dreading that funeral shop

"Thoughts and prayers" are no real consolation.
No one ever fathoms the mental or emotional isolation
When they try to marry knowledge and time through twisted desolation
... a blood oath's consummation

Throwing off balance the universal laws;
Interrupting someone's purposed cause...
Because your disgruntled feelings never gave pause
To the lives you'd affect through planned applause

CLAP! CLAP! CLAP! No hands, but the sound of bullets
Was the last ovation someone heard after you pulled it...
That trigger, with an angry intent and simple finger.
What mental triggers caused your apathetic demeanor?

Dedicated to the victims of the 5/31/19 Virginia Beach massacre... may your souls find peace and karmic vengeance

Graduation Celebration

I didn't think I would ever finish...
Started four years ago, but after two, hopes kinda diminished.
Personal things and situations got in the way
But hey, that was what I assumed of life's sway
I'd experienced the black and white; but this grey...
This unknown territory really tested by strength from day to day
Had my mind in poor to Mint Condition... nothing left to say.
But perseverance would not let me falter
Had to lay it all on a Universal altar
A load bigger and heavier than Gibraltar.
I put myself back into the game;
It was now for a different reason and not the same.
Not just for knowledge and elevation,
But real and true soul salvation!
Who knew I would find myself through continued education
By way of life application?
And it's sooooo amazin!!
And YES! As of today, I can say I did it!
I've completed one degree but have rotated a full 360!
Oops, fear and doubt, you missed me!

FREE DOME (Freedom)

Out with the old! In with the new
Throwing out old speech and bad habits I used to do
Obtaining new knowledge and a new mindset
Those former shackles of mental bondage will I soon forget
This sun represents my brain power
Activated rays of truth onto the world I'll shower
Fuck your stories and your allegories!
Extra! Extra! There's been a shift in my priorities!
I now only extract from conscientious quarries –
Digging the crystals from the lake like Jason Voorhees
Slicing and dicing into misconceptions and lies;
Killing any rhetoric or mind games the elite tries
Oh yes! My mind has been super-sized
And the deceit now exorcised
That's what true freedom is...
When your cerebral thoughts reflect that square biz
When the light emanating from you shines bright
And strikes that universal palette just right
My soul no longer looks for a house, but has found home
All because I decided to pursue a free dome!

Return to Glory

I was afraid to step into the darkness
Tried reasoning with my mind as to what started this
And what should've been fear, turned to bliss
What was once light, now turned into memories remiss

The realization that everything had been flipped
All of a sudden made me wanna rewrite the script
Discarding all the lies... all the deceit
And fade back into dark shadows discreet

Into the blackness, from whence all things came
Where substance, matter, intellect, and energy were all one in the same...
Into the blackness we've been taught to fear and shame...
What I now embrace will most definitely change the game!

For out of this darkness burst a marvelous and superior light!
The supernova of right knowledge encapsulating my third eye's sight!
Out of chaos, came supreme order;
My consciousness level risen to new heights!

Elevation in every sense of the word and definition;
Pineal flying as high as a falcon, cresting towards the Sun, of its own volition.
Star gazing by my own admission
The sole goal now being righteous ascension
Into the spiritually awakened dimension!

Now that it all makes sense, and nothing remains the same,
It's only right that I return to the darkness from whence I came.
No longer the thought of just a melanated story;
This trip right here... is definitely a return to glory!

Bird Box

Blinded from birth
She moves gracefully and effortlessly through life
Although she can't physically see,
Her third eye and sixth sense guide her walk
She has strategically built her nesting place...
Firm, secure, and nurturing
Her mind is open and closed at the same time
Optimistic, yet guarded... wisdom becoming her crown
Her countenance and words are sweet solace
Radiance springs out of her into the atmosphere
And now I know why the caged bird sings

Baby Birth

My soul was being prepped for travel;
First class flight from the 5th dimension to the third.
Once in a lifetime chance of experiences unheard.
The Creator already slammed the gavel.

So I previewed what I'd be dealing with;
No need to say I was appalled by the view!
I quickly shouted, "Oh hell naw! God, what do you want ME to do?"
"Represent me, child... make truth out of myth."

A huge task for such a small world, I thought;
Yet, I could see my purpose unfolding before my eyes.
Turning hate to love, brewing happiness from defeated cries.
A mirrored image of my now, a reflection of here, I sought.

And so I went, with nervous courage and apprehension;
And that was shown once I arrived and was delivered.
It wasn't the cold, but the uncertainty in why I cried and shivered.
Now an alien, called human; birthed into a lower dimension.

I See Things Differently

I closed real eyes to realize the world's deceptions
Opened up my third eye and gained a different perception...
While they march to a different drumbeat,
I float on the sweet tunes of the piper's treat
Disinformation and corruption, I try to defeat
But it's hard to combat infamous tweets
And with ignorance no longer being discreet
I just close my eyes to the deceit
My pineal is open and aware
Into other dimensions I stare
My mind becomes clear and bare
Refreshed with wisdom from Out There
Discernment and knowledge pave my path with care...
I know... therefore I am... I can smile while you blankly stare.

The Good, The Bad, The Ugly

Gorgeous gals and gentle gents going
Over opulent obstacles ostentatiously showing
Gathering giggles while germinating gigs
Jostling through central park, jovial jogs and jigs
It was a GOOD day...

Then the turn of time transfigured to terror
Soot and smoke solicited signals of error
Rubble rolled and rumbled towards humanity
No one cared to save a life, only to text, film, and
tweet
We were in a BAD way...

Senseless and sordid shots of sin-ematography
Blatant bombs over Baghdad begat bogus weapons of
biology
Smokescreen became thicker, while cell phones
became bigger and quicker
Lost sight of the real picture
Becoming iPhone and Android cotton pickers
... for the sake of a flicker...
Such an UGLY display...

What's In a Name?

If you call yourself a Queen or a King, you betta think bigger...
If you prefer to be addressed as a Goddess or a God, you've got much more to consider
And you ask me, "My nigga... how do you figure?!"
It's so complicatedly simple... but it's easy to see
Because our cosmically galactic melanin proves we are more than royalty or deity.
We started this shit – we gone end this shit
Cuz our very essence transcends all time tick...
Tock... Ticktok Ticktok...
Our clock never stops
We are recycled thru this plane until ascension knocks
"Shouldn't I realize... you're the highest of the high... if you don't know, then I'll say it..."
<cough> <cough> Ahem – not that Maxwell ish
See, I'm serving a different dish
Something sacred to self-care and preservation
Feeding the mind and soul thru chakric delegation
Kundalini rising like a phoenix from the sacrum to the crown...
Toroidal spins 360 degrees around;
The ancestral, astrological language have I found!!
So, you betta believe that your rhetoric will not cast or weigh me down.
Trendsetters! We're just better
Following trends should we never!
Always and forever the Pinnacle...
Whether thru culture, sports, fashion, or these words lyrical
We achieve ALL things that seem dynastic or empirical!
Time after time, we're the best of the best

Especially when put to the test;
And stand fearlessly at the precipice
On the edge of this plane that we call Earth...
True guardians of the galaxy – defenders of the hearth.
So, be addressed in your right and proper Divinity
Because our cosmically galactic melanin, and righteous ancient history
Proves we are so much more than royalty or deity!!

Breaking Spells

I've been reborn and set free
Released from the spells that shackled me!
Adjudicated in life and liberty
To summon the powers of my own manifest destiny.
I've cried... I've fought... I've learned... and I've taught
Nothing prepares you for the pleasures or pains brought
When you decide to let go of every conceivable and mustered thought
Trying to avoid the numerous rabbit holes... fearing you could get caught
Up up and away into a world wide web of disinformation
Crawling and scraping thru hordes of indoctrination
Just to attempt to do your part to help doctor a nation
To obtain right knowledge, you may call that brilliance
But to make that knowledge kinetic, I'll call that resilience!
I move and think different
My walk and talk you may think is belligerent -
And to that thought I give my entire consent
Cuz we're indeed at all-out war in this day and age
Smoked filled rooms, sound bowls and sage
I embrace the true Lady of Rage -
The Big Momma energy that seeks vengeance for her child
Fuck "Girls..." This is "Source Gone Wild"
In being part of Source, I am therefore a Sourceror!
So I bind and cast against negative negativity
Empower these chakras with inherent transmissibility
Firing shots against your dogma and indoctrinations
I'm hell bent on restoring retribution to the nations

When they told me to get closer to God,
I just hugged myself a little tighter...
And like Thanos with the snap of the finger, I
changed my reality for brighter.
I am eclectic versatility - electrical beauty - a magnet's
duty
Giving charge to both positive and negative ions
Polar opposition, a rare phenomenon
A once in a lifetime generational scion
I am a modern Marvel...
But don't you dare mis-take me as a comic book
character -
Although I am the archetype and prototype that they
were molded after
The real and true Incredible Hulk;
Absorbing the sun's gamma radiation in bulk
I'm the Ironman - savvy and sarcastic dialect
Paired with speed, agility, strength, and genius
intellect.
I'm an abracadabra Avenger!
My words penetrate the fabric of space and time!
They transform the multiverse ether at the drop of a
dime!
Highly influenced by the powers of the 3... the 6... and
the 9
Yeah, I'm on my Tesla shit via majestic design
I've broken the old spell and cast a new one over my
reality to shine
It's about damn time you do the same and trust
yourself to follow that magickal spine... that pineal
vine... That Kundalini serpentine line!
RISE!!!
RISE!!!
RISE!!!

Self-Discovery

In the journey of self-discovery, I tread,
A path of whispers, where emotions are spread.
Through mists of uncertainty, I seek to find,
The essence of my soul, the depths of my mind.

With every step, I peel back the layers,
Unveiling truths, confronting my fears.
In the mirror of introspection, I gaze,
A canvas of memories, where moments blaze.

Fairness to myself, a promise I make,
To cherish my worth, and not forsake.
For in the tapestry of life, I find,
The threads of self-love intricately twined.

I learn to forgive, to let go of regret,
To embrace imperfections, not to forget,
That growth comes from struggles, battles within,
And embracing my flaws, where healing begins.

Through valleys of darkness, I find the light,
A beacon of hope, shining so bright.
I discover passions that fuel my soul,
A tapestry of dreams carefully unrolls.

Fairness, like a compass, guides my way,
A North Star of kindness in every sway.
To honor my needs, my desires, my heart,
To paint my own canvas, a work of art.

In the symphony of self-discovery's song,
I harmonize with purpose, where I belong.

The journey continues, a lifelong quest,
To be fair to myself, and to always be my best.

Perfect Fit

The pieces I'm made of are fragile.
Brittle, malleable even... there's no denial.
Yet, I still exude love, whether through kiss or touch
It's just more cautionary now... doesn't take much
For the slightest tinker to break me into pieces;
And my soul to return to you what it releases.
Spiritual glue keeps this puzzle together
Burdens and trials of life become light as a feather
And I deeply wait to exhale and wonder whether
Today will be triumphant and so much better.
Eyes closed, I wish upon a star
For the day where "I am" becomes "We are."
I know the love you offer will finally make me complete
I'm just waiting for our destinies to align and meet
Whoever you are, I'm waiting for your healing
Come soon, so my heart can stop reeling
And my soul can once again gain feeling
Of what it's like to again have match-made dealings
My body is a chess board... and I await your checkmate, King.

Signed,
A Broken But Optimistic Queen

Family First

Family! Ain't nothing like it!
When it comes to unconditional, we're love's true pundits
And best believe I adore and cherish all 88 hunnit!
You laugh at that number, but it's close to true
Can't go NOWHERE without bumping into a cousin or two!
Whether close or distant in blood relation,
You could never tell because we act unified as one nation
Under God, indivisible we are, near or far
See, it don't have to be Christmas cold or summertime warm;
It's a 365 feeling... that's why it's tattooed on my arm
And they'll always come first!
Like a new morning's sunburst
Anticipated refreshment
Of memories collected
Like streets in the city – we're all connected!
Even the additions and extensions
Don't go without me making mention
Of their inclusive intentions.
My family doesn't just rock the world, we rock dimensions!

AP2P
(a collaboration with Michael "Po'etech" Morris)

All power to the people!
I shout it from the tallest steeple!
So this voice can echo across the land,
Reaching folk from here to Japan
Oxymoron upon similes upon metaphors
This pen floods many pages when it pours
Flow is so insane
They nicknamed me Crazy Brain
As lyrical and fresh as Big Daddy Kane
Yet as smooth and mellow as Candy Rain
...and my Soul is for Real!
These lines are kinda like a big deal
My life's passion in plain black and white
And just like the police, these words gone strike
Pierce your mind like a black thief in the night
Maybe not even give a fuck, and come for you in the daylight
"Hands up! Don't shoot," they say
But I gotta spit these bars and try to relay
This message, injected into your system like crack needles
Refuel and recharge your conscience
So that one day, you yourself can shout ALL POWER TO THE PEOPLE!

Just prayed for wisdom like Solomon
The king had a dream like Martin
To resuscitate the hip hop populace
I filled up every phrase like a bottle of oxygen
Frustrated with all these debates and arguments
My people still sleepwalking and marching
It's hard to raise a mind state full of toxic jargon

Listening to politicians spit all that garbage
Sitting behind bars like Mumia Abu-Jamal
Freedom's my call!
Giving the government a rude awakening
Even without pardon
We all need a change of pace
Cause this world will wear you down
Like models walking in heavy garments
They say life is short
But I've been ready to live it up for the longest
For hours I sit, meditating til I'm peaceful
Contemplating Love and War
Like Tamar in beast mode
My Sunday Cipher bars
Shout ALL POWER TO THE PEOPLE
While y'all watch the "Empire" fall from evil
I'm making moves like Ghost
In that "Power" sequel
Spittin' lethal flames from my brain
Like a Desert Eagle...
Good morning y'all
ALL POWER TO THE PEOPLE!

PUBLIC NOTICE

This is a public notice of tribal origin.

Designation and application: For the collective benefit of ALL clans, knowing or unknowing, of the tribal mothers' right to assert as tribal rite the restoration of The Great Law; the Grandmother Clause and Mothers' right to serve and protect the offspring of herself and all other mothers similarly situated.

I am **(NAME HERE)**, mother and matriarch with direct blood ties to the Earth and the first earth inhabitants; called in modern science "Genus Homo" or "Sapien Sapien." The root to the matrix being mitochondria – and I as mother, along with other mothers are authorized by Prime Creator to regulate our species DNA by mitochondrial analysis of "Y" chromosomes to heal, correct, repair, and host those who carry the "Y" chromosome as responsible fashioners of future generations of men by divine decree and order.

As our Ancestors spoke into existence all that existed, We the mothers of the Earth tribes speaking for Mother Earth, channeling Prime Creator through a pure heart, clear mind, and direct link through "Life's All Portal" – called in modern terms the uterus/womb and mystically as the "Portal of Life" that all children, male and female, must come through as children of the Earth, Sun, Moon, and Stars – manifest as sentient beings endowed with the genetic code to always restore, maintain, and support a balanced life as a caretaker of the Earth and teachers of all humanity.

We now speak the great liberation of all clans, tribes, and families – called in modern law by misnomers of "nationals, citizens, voters, and the public." Given faux/false names to intentionally and with malice and aforethought, mislead all the Earth tribes into the unconscious surrender of birthright, inheritance, and sovereign standing before all tribes. With a Mother's stern rejection, I (and We) say ENOUGH!!

We call for a definite and clear end to public displays of deception and privately held secrets designed to usurp the natural given inalienable rights of any and all clans, clan members, and their respective leadership, whom the legal fiction has derailed and undermined from fulfilling tribal functions and proper administration of tribal law.

I, **(NAME HERE)**, call to life and call to light ALL Chiefs being bound, restricted, captured, and held captive. Also, informing by public notice, timestamped, and dated in archivable format, before all clans across the land according to our tribal tradition of the spoken law, with neither acknowledgement nor approval being needed from the legal fiction (which is now defunct), formerly known as The United States Incorporated.

It is by superior jurisdiction and competent discourse I, and other clan mothers inform the tribes of the orders in agreement with the collective tribes, to return to our tribal ways; asserting our oral tradition and inalienable rites to return all clans back to The Great Law, without delay nor obstruction. This is my notice. This is my decree. Publicly announcing the returning Matriarchy and a new beginning across the lands.

Quotes 'N' Notes:
Thinking, Reflecting,
and Journaling

Each new day is our chance to regroup, reform, and refocus from yesterday's trials and errors, mistakes, and blurred vision. Be thankful you got a fresh start! #newleaseonlife

"Morning by morning, new mercies I see…" Every new day encountered should begin with positivity and thankfulness. It is an opportunity we all tend to take for granted; and we assume and plan to see the next day to carry out dreams and hopes of betterment. However, it is not promised to us. Living in the NOW is where it's at! It has been said that the past, present, and future all exist simultaneously. What if that is true? If that is indeed so, then today at this very moment, we can very well choose to regroup from our past (yesterday/yesteryear), reform our present, and refocus or realign our goals for the future all simultaneously! Reflection on the past, and projection towards the future are both wise and optimistic. But the culmination of both exists only in the present and personal choices we make - hence, a true gift.

The true test is not in being able to withstand the storm, but how to handle and what to do in the aftermath of it. #assessment #totality #whenyousurvive #butnothingelsedid

Many times over, we have been taught to "weather the storm." Philosophically or religiously, this seems to showcase strength and endurance through hard times. Although it is a great and motivational phrase, it can tend to lead one to a dead end of false hope and no follow through. What about after the storm? From where do the final assessment and cost of damages derive? It is only after these steps that healing, recovery, and rebuilding can occur. You cannot see the totality of damage done while in your storm. The clouds must break apart for the sun to shine, the water must recede to see dry ground again; things must be shifted and moved out of the way to ensure additional life was not lost. Assessment after the storm is the real test. Herein lies the intestinal fortitude in whether to continue pushing forward, or to throw in the towel in defeat. The anchor will keep you grounded and in place during the storm - but it is of no good use to you if after a storm the anchor is left as just a standalone monument or paperweight. Let it be your testament and stronghold even AFTER!

Holding on to setbacks and mistakes of the past not only hurts others, it also hurts YOU because it blinds you to forward progression. You can’ t see change if you’ re not looking for it… moving like pond water, and pond water doesn’ t move! #stopstagnation #letitgo

The saying, “Hurt people, hurt people…” holds to be so true. Internalizing anger, depression, disappointment, or wrongdoing without a proper outlet of reconciliation damages the spirit and character of who you are while simultaneously destroying bonds with others. In those negative states of consciousness, we can tend to get stuck in a cycle of continuous and repetitive bondage. Bondage within that holds us captive against forgiveness. The most important step in moving forward, is to first forgive yourself. Progression cannot take place unless we start to heal our inner sanctum before dealing with outside company and situations. And the goal is to do so quickly, so that there is no time for the negativity to fester inside! This is how you grow and ascend into higher realms of self-knowledge, self-confidence, and self-worth. It is only when you begin to look within that you will find all that you have been looking for; so work on removing the hurt so the path can be made clearer, and obfuscation can turn to clarification.

Life would be so much simpler, easier, and less stressful if we only stopped to evaluate OURSELVES, admit to our OWN wrongdoings, faults, shortcomings, misgivings, preconceptions, prejudices… and after admitting them, own up to them, accept them, and CHANGE them for the better! It doesn't just stop at realizing the problem! PROaction is required! Only then will a new YOU emerge from the dying flower you once were! #admittanceisgood #changeisbetter #4seasonsignificance

This quote beautifully encapsulates the idea that personal growth and self-improvement are essential components while embarking on a journey of self-discovery. Introspection is a most valuable tool that very few use yet is highly important. For through this gift, we can admit, accept, own, and change what we deem to be our flaws. However, we must even change our thinking of "flawedness." In duality, we must view both polarities of a thing - not in terms of said thing being either good or bad; but seeking to balance the poles. There is no one without the other, so we must make proper use of the whole instead of viewing only one side. Think of introspection as you viewing your whole self, and then balancing out your pros and cons to create a more efficient YOU!

The best relationships come from sacrifices, not convenience or comfortability; from mistakes made and learned from, not perfection; from vulnerabilities and transparencies, not pride and closed hearts or minds.

Relationships often require sacrifices, whether it's your time, personal preferences, or even your own comfort. When you're willing to make sacrifices for someone, it shows your commitment and dedication to the relationship's growth and well-being. Convenience and comfort, while enjoyable, can sometimes lead to complacency. Sacrifices, on the other hand, demonstrate a willingness to go the extra mile for your partner or loved ones.

Perfection is an unrealistic standard. In any relationship, people will make mistakes. What's important is how you both handle those mistakes. Learning from them and using them as opportunities for growth and improvement can strengthen a relationship. It's through these shared experiences that you develop resilience and a deeper understanding of each other.

Vulnerability and transparency are key to building trust and intimacy. When you open up to someone about your fears, insecurities, and emotions, you create a space for genuine connection. Pride and closed hearts or minds can create barriers that prevent meaningful communication and understanding. It's essential to be willing to lower these barriers and be authentic with your other-self - for you are, indeed, reflections of one another.

Life is feminine, and living is masculine… both energies must blend together to achieve maximum potential.

In this context, "life" is described as feminine, which may imply qualities such as nurturing, creativity, receptivity, and a sense of interconnectedness. It could be seen as the essence or force that sustains and gives birth to all things. This perspective likens life to the concept of a mother or a source of energy and creation. On the other hand, "living" is characterized as masculine; suggesting qualities such as action, assertiveness, vigor, and the act of actively engaging with the world. It could be viewed as the way individuals interact with and shape their existence through their choices and actions. This perspective likens living to the role of a father or an active force in the world.

The idea behind this statement is that for a person to realize their full potential and experience a harmonious and fulfilling life, they should combine both the qualities associated with "life" (feminine) and "living" (masculine). This blending of energies represents a balanced approach to existence:

To achieve one's maximum potential, one should balance qualities like receptivity, creativity, and nurturing (life) with qualities like action, determination, and engagement (living). This perspective suggests that embracing both aspects is essential for holistic growth and self-fulfillment. It encourages one to integrate aspects of contemplation, introspection, and nurturing (feminine) with proactive decision-making, effort, and action (masculine). By recognizing that both energies are necessary, individuals can achieve a sense of wholeness and completeness in their lives. They can find meaning and purpose by not only being receptive to life's experiences but also actively shaping their path. They represent archetypal energies or principles that can be found in all individuals, regardless of gender.

Although they can be interpreted or construed differently, words, once they come off the lips, can be forgiven but never taken back or forgotten. #choosewisely

Words are not always straightforward and may have various interpretations or meanings. What one person says may be understood differently by someone else, depending on their perspective, context, and personal experiences.

The irreversible nature of spoken words are indeed spells cast. Once words are spoken aloud, they cannot be erased or withdrawn. People may forgive the speaker for their words, but they cannot be erased from memory, and their effects can linger. In essence,
"choose wisely" is a call to action. It encourages one to be thoughtful and deliberate when choosing their words before speaking. Consider the potential consequences and interpretations of what you are about to say. How are you wielding your power with words?

Achievement shall NOT be confinement! You are limitless in your potential! After every milestone, there is STILL work to do!

Achieving a goal or milestone should not limit or confine you. In other words, reaching a particular level of success should not make you complacent or restrict your ambitions. Instead, it suggests that accomplishment should be a stepping stone to greater things, not a barrier that holds you back.

Your potential is boundless; and your human capabilities are not limited! You have the capacity to keep growing, learning, and achieving more, regardless of your past accomplishments. Even after achieving a significant goal, there will always be more challenges to tackle and new milestones to reach. Be encouraged in perseverance, ongoing effort, and the recognition that personal and professional development is a lifelong process.

“A teacher is never a giver of the truth; they are a guide - a pointer to a truth that each student must find for themselves.” - Bruce Lee

A teacher’s role is to lead students on a journey of discovery and learning. Teachers provide direction, support, and resources to help students navigate the complex world of knowledge. Truth is not something that can be handed over or imposed on someone. It's not a ready-made product that a teacher can deliver to a student. Instead, truth is something that each individual must actively seek and uncover through their own efforts and experiences. Learning is a proactive and participatory process. Students must engage with the subject matter, think critically about it, question assumptions, and apply their own intellect to arrive at a deeper understanding of the truth. This active engagement in the learning process is essential for meaningful knowledge acquisition.

Keeping in mind the individual perspective, truth can be subjective and may vary from person to person. What is true for one may not be the same for another. Teachers help students develop their own perspectives and interpretations of truth based on their unique experiences and insights. Education does not end in the classroom but continues throughout one's life as individuals continue to seek and discover new truths.

YOUR STORY DOESN' T END WITH WHAT YOU' VE BEEN THROUGH! IT ONLY BEGINS WITH WHAT YOU PLAN ON DOING! #createanewyou

Everyone has a history and has faced various challenges, hardships, and experiences in their past. However, your past does not define you or limit your potential. Your past is just a part of your story, but it is not the final chapter. Forward-thinking and planning for the future is an ongoing process, and is determined by the actions, choices, and plans you make today. Be encouraged to set goals, make positive changes, and take the steps toward creating a better and more fulfilling life. You have the power to reinvent yourself, transform your life, and become the person you aspire to be. So, break free from the constraints of your past, overcome adversity, and focus on the opportunities and possibilities that lie ahead. Promote a mindset of resilience, determination, and the belief that you have the ability to shape your own destiny by taking action and creating a new and better version of yourself.

Re-evaluating circumstances in your life is a key tool to growth. Assessing your life situation(s) and then moving forward in a positive way only opens doors to success and blessings. Never say you're stuck with a problem… if the right Source is leading you, and your mind is focused, there will ALWAYS be a solution!

A key tool to growth is periodically taking a step back and reflecting on your life's situations and experiences. This act of self-assessment and reflection allows you to take stock of where you are in various aspects of your life, such as your career, relationships, personal goals, and overall well-being. This self-examination allows you to gain a deeper understanding of your current circumstances, strengths, weaknesses, and areas that may need improvement. Once you have identified areas in your life that require attention or improvement, you should take necessary steps to make positive changes. This can involve setting goals, making necessary adjustments, or seeking new opportunities that align with your aspirations. Success and blessings are viewed as potential rewards for those who are willing to self-reflect and work towards improvement.

Most people don’t want to wake up to reality because it destroys and decimates their illusion or perception of life; and what is life to you? Is it that which you’ve been on this earth plane? Is it the culmination of experiences? Or is it something far greater that we’ve had yet to experience due to suppression? How would it make you feel to know you have been walking blindly on this journey your entire lifespan? But comfortability keeps you in that state of mind. Just know that, that comfort is about to be shaken to the very core of your being… brace yourself, steady your feet, protect and feed your energies, and open your spirit to change – because change and difference is DEFINITELY coming!!

Other Notes and Reflections

Made in the USA
Columbia, SC
09 June 2025

59082486R00100